I'm the Chef!

I'm the Chef!

Crabtree Publishing Company

PMB 16A, 350 Fifth Avenue
Suite 3308, New York,
NY 10118

612 Welland Avenue,
St. Catharines, Ontario
Canada L2M 5V6

Created by **McRae Books**

Copyright © McRae Books Srl, 2001

Coordinating Editor: Ellen Rodger
Project Editor: Lisa Gurusinghe
Production Coordinator: Rosie Gowsell
Production Assistance: Mary-Anne Luzba
Consulting Chef: Dan Fudge

McRae Books Srl.
Project Manager: Anne McRae
Texts: Rosalba Gioffrè
Editors: Holly Willis, Anne McRae
Photography: Marco Lanza, Walter Mericchi
Set Design: Rosalba Gioffrè
Design: Marco Nardi
Layout and cutouts: Laura Ottina, Adriano Nardi
Special thanks to: Mastrociliegia (Fiesole), and Dino Bartolini (Florence), who kindly lent props for photography..
Picture credits: p. 23 Gentile da Fabriano, *The Three Kings*, Uffizi (Florence) / Scala Group, Florence.
Color separations: Fotolito Toscana, Florence, Italy

CATALOGING-IN-PUBLICATION DATA

Gioffre, Rosalba.
  The Young Chef's French cookbook / Rosalba Gioffre [sic.].
    p. cm. -- (I'm the chef)
  Includes index.
  ISBN 0-7787-0282-0 (RLB) -- ISBN 0-7787-0296-0 (pbk.)
  1. Cookery, French--Juvenile literature. 2. Quick and easy
cookery--Juvenile literature. [1. Cookery, French.]   I. Title. II.
Series.
  TX719 .G56 2001
  641.5944--dc21
                00-065995
                LC

123456789 Printed and bound in Italy - Nuova GEP   987654321

I'm the Chef!

The Young Chef's
FRENCH
COOKBOOK

🌳 **Crabtree**
www.crabtreebooks.com

List of Contents

Introduction

French food is so good that it has become famous all over the world. Despite its reputation as a complicated **cuisine**, there are many dishes that young chefs can prepare successfully. In this book, there are 15 classic recipes with step-by-step photographs. Follow the instructions carefully and you will be able to serve your friends and family delicious meals. Each recipe has special tips and tricks to help you get it right from the start. The central pages (pp. 22–23) focus on The Feast of the Kings, a festival that children in France celebrate on January 6. So, enjoy, or as the French say, *Bon appétit!*

Croque-Monsieur

Toasted cheese and ham sandwich

This toasted sandwich was invented in a bar on the Boulevard des Capucines in Paris in 1910. Not only is it tasty, but this sandwich is "a breeze" to make. A sort of French fast food, you can make a number of variations of this sandwich. Try topping it with a fried egg. In this case it is called a croque- Madame!

1 Leave the butter to soften at room temperature. It should be soft but not melted. Use a spatula or bread knife to spread it onto one side of the bread.

2 Grate the cheese. Be sure to keep your fingertips well away from the grater.

TIPS & TRICKS

Ask an adult to help you when putting the croque-Monsieur into, or taking it out of the oven. If you do it yourself, be sure to wear thick oven mitts to protect your hands.

Ingredients

1 tablespoon
(15 ml) butter

2 slices bread

1 oz (30 g)
Gruyère or
Swiss cheese

2 slices
of ham

3 Cover one of the slices of bread with two slices of ham. **Trim** off any extra ham and place it in the middle. **Sprinkle** the grated cheese over the ham.

When you add the cheese, place most of it in the center of the sandwich to stop it from coming out when cooking.

Utensils

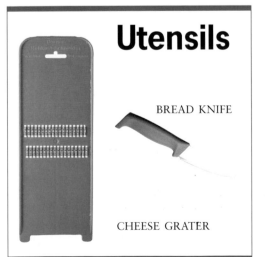

BREAD KNIFE

CHEESE GRATER

4 Place the other slice of bread on top, with the buttered side facing inward. Cook the croque-Monsieur in a preheated oven at 350°F (180°C) for about 15 minutes, or until nicely browned on both sides.

Crêpe au fromage
Cheese crêpes

Crêpes are one of the most famous of French dishes, so to be a real French chef you must learn how to make them. Luckily, they are not very difficult. Crêpes can be served with salty fillings, such as cheese and ham, or with sweet ones, such as sugar, jam, chocolate, and whipped cream. Even today, there are crêpe stalls on many street corners in Paris and other cities in France.

TIPS & TRICKS

Each time you add batter to the skillet, add a little more melted butter first. Hold the skillet firmly by the handle as you cook the crêpes. If you do not have **Gruyère cheese**, *use a thin slice of cheddar cheese, or any other kind that melts well, in its place.*

Utensils

SKILLET (FRYING PAN)

MIXING BOWL

EGG BEATER

WHISK

SLOTTED SPATULA

Ingredients

1¼ cups (300 ml) all-purpose plain flour

Dash of salt

1 cup (250 ml) milk

2 eggs

2½ tablespoons (35 ml) butter

8 thin slices Gruyère or other cheese

8 thin slices ham

6 Return the folded crêpes to the pan long enough to melt the cheese. Serve them warm.

1 **Sift** the flour and salt into a bowl. Pour in the milk a little at a time, stirring continuously with a whisk or fork.

2 Stirring continuously, add the eggs one at a time, followed by the butter. The mixture should be smooth and well mixed. Place in the refrigerator for one hour.

3 Melt a little butter in a 9-inch (22 cm) **skillet** and add a **ladleful** of batter.

4 Move the skillet back and forth so that a thin layer of batter covers the bottom evenly. Cook until light brown on one side. Use a slotted spatula to flip, and cook the other side. Repeat until all the batter is cooked.

5 Cover half of each crêpe with a slice of cheese and a slice of ham. Fold the empty half over the top.

Place the crêpes on a preheated serving dish. Serve with a green salad for lunch.

Gratin de macaroni
Baked macaroni with béchamel

Béchamel is a basic and well known French white sauce. It was invented by Louis de Béchamel, who was head **butler** at the grand court of King Louis XIV in the 17th century. Béchamel goes particularly well with pasta, but is also delicious with vegetables baked in the oven.

Utensils

CHEESE GRATER

COLANDER

WOODEN SPOON

SAUCEPAN

OVENPROOF BAKING DISH

1 Melt the butter in a saucepan over low heat. Remove from the heat and sift in the flour, stirring continuously so that no lumps form.

2 Return to the heat and cook for 1–2 minutes, so that the flour is lightly "toasted."

3 Pour in the milk a little at a time, stirring continuously. Add salt, pepper, and nutmeg to taste. After a few minutes, the mixture will boil. Cook for 3-4 minutes, stirring continuously.

4 Lightly butter an ovenproof dish and cover the bottom with a layer of cooked pasta. Curl the long strands around to cover the dish as evenly as you can. You can also use other types of pasta, short or long.

5 Cover the pasta with a layer of béchamel, followed by a layer of Gruyère and a sprinkling of Parmesan. Repeat until all the ingredients are used up.

Ingredients

 ½ cup (125 ml) butter

7 tablespoons (105 ml) all-purpose/ plain flour

Salt and black pepper

dash of freshly grated nutmeg

 2 cups (500 ml) warm milk

10 oz (300 g) precooked ziti pasta

5 oz (150 g) Gruyère cheese

 ¼ cup (60 ml) freshly grated Parmesan cheese

TIPS & TRICKS

To cook the pasta, place a large pot of lightly salted cold water over high heat. When it is boiling, add the pasta and cook for the time indicated on the package. When the pasta is cooked, ask an adult to help you drain it in the colander.

6 Preheat oven at 400°F (200°C) and bake for about 20 minutes, or until a golden crust, or 'gratin' has formed. Ask an adult to remove the hot dish and serve straight from the oven.

Omelette aux tomates
Tomato omelet

Omelets are quick and easy to make. They are also **nutritious** and fun to serve. They can be eaten plain, with herbs, or filled with cheese, tomatoes, ham, or any of your favorite ingredients. Omelets are also practical when unexpected friends drop by. If eggs are the only food you have in your refrigerator, you can offer them this delicious treat.

Ingredients

1 red onion

4 ripe tomatoes

2 tablespoons (30 ml) olive oil

salt and ground black pepper

6 eggs

1 bunch parsley

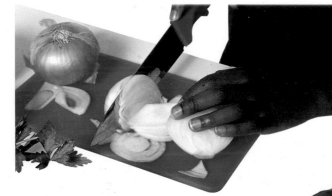

1 On a chopping board, slice the onion in thin wheels with a sharp knife. Hold the knife firmly by the handle, and keep your fingers well away from the blade. Ask an adult to help.

TIPS & TRICKS

While cooking the omelet, make sure that the skillet handle does not stick out. You might bump it onto yourself or the floor as you pass by the stove.

2 Place a pot of water over high heat. When the water boils, turn off the heat and carefully add the tomatoes. Leave for 2 minutes, then remove with a slotted spoon. When the tomatoes have cooled down, remove the skins with your fingers. **Chop** the tomatoes into tiny pieces.

Utensils

CHOPPING BOARD

KNIFE

SKILLET (FRYING PAN)

WOODEN SPATULA

3 Heat the oil in a skillet and add the onion and tomato. Season with salt and pepper and cook over medium to low heat for 15 minutes. Stir from time to time. Hold the handle of the skillet while you stir with a wooden spatula.

4 Break the eggs into a bowl and beat them quickly with a fork. Season with a little salt.

5 Lightly oil a nonstick skillet and place over medium to low heat. Pour in half the eggs and cook for 4–5 minutes. Move the skillet gently side to side as the omelet cooks. Remove the omelet from the heat and slide it onto a serving dish.

6 Cook the second omelet as shown above. Pour half the tomato sauce onto one half of each omelet, sprinkle with chopped parsley, and use a wooden spatula to fold it in two.

Quiche Lorraine
Quiche with bacon

The word quiche comes from the German word *Kuchen*, which means **savory** pie or tart. There are many different types of quiche, but quiche Lorraine is the classic one. It was invented by a French cook in the northern city of Nancy in the 16th century. The French serve quiche as a **first course**, but it is so filling and nourishing that it can be served as a meal in itself.

1 Sift the flour and salt into a mixing bowl. Add the chopped butter and work it in using your fingers until the mixture is the **consistency** of bread crumbs. Gradually pour in the water and mix until the dough is smooth and elastic. Shape it into a ball and leave in the refrigerator for 30 minutes.

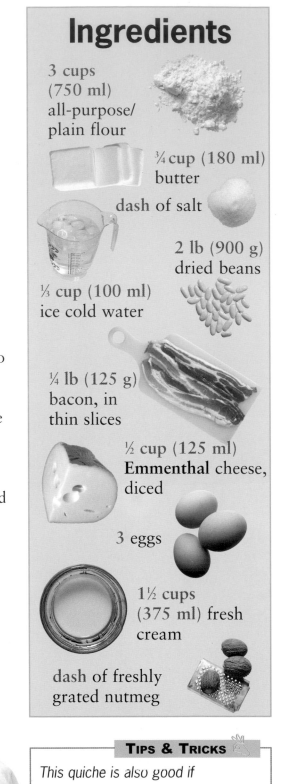

Ingredients

3 cups (750 ml) all-purpose/plain flour

¾ cup (180 ml) butter

dash of salt

⅓ cup (100 ml) ice cold water

2 lb (900 g) dried beans

¼ lb (125 g) bacon, in thin slices

½ cup (125 ml) **Emmenthal** cheese, diced

3 eggs

1½ cups (375 ml) fresh cream

dash of freshly grated nutmeg

TIPS & TRICKS

This quiche is also good if made with ham instead of bacon. Ask an adult to help when putting dishes in, or taking them out of the oven and remember to use oven mitts.

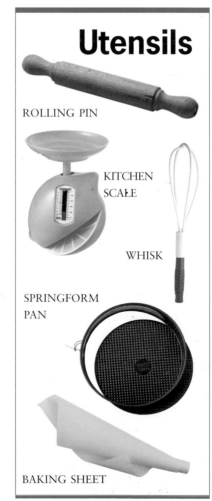

2 Lightly flour a rolling pin and roll the dough out on a floured work surface until it is about ¼ inch (5 mm) thick.

3 Use the dough to line a buttered and floured 10-inch (26-cm) diameter **springform pan.**

4 Prick the dough on the bottom of the pan with a fork. Cover with a sheet of ovenproof paper and fill with the dried beans. Bake in a preheated oven at 400°F (200°C) for 20 minutes.

Utensils

ROLLING PIN

KITCHEN SCALE

WHISK

SPRINGFORM PAN

BAKING SHEET

5 Remove the baked pastry shell from the oven and throw away the paper and beans. Brown the bacon slightly and line the bottom with it. Sprinkle with the cheese.

6 Beat the eggs and cream with a whisk. Add a dash of salt and nutmeg. Pour the mixture over the bacon and cheese. Bake in a preheated oven at 350°F (180°C) for 30 minutes.

Salade niçoise

Tuna, egg, and tomato salad

This healthy, colorful salad is easy to prepare and requires almost no cooking. Served with freshly baked French bread, this salad makes a nutritious lunch or snack. Its name comes from Nice, a beautiful city on the Mediterranean Sea in the south of France. Many fish dishes are unique to this region. The ingredients can be changed so that if you do not like onions, for example, you can replace them with another herb or vegetable.

1 Wash the vegetables and dry them thoroughly. Slice the red pepper across the middle and remove the seeds and core. Slice it into thin, round strips.

2 Peel and slice the cucumber into thin pieces. Cut the tomatoes into thin **wedges** and the onion into thin wheels. Place the lettuce leaves in a salad bowl.

Utensils

SALAD BOWL

CUTTING BOARD

KNIFE

4 Sprinkle with a little salt and drizzle with the oil. Use salad tongs to toss the ingredients. Be sure to do this carefully so that the eggs do not break up.

3 Peel the eggs and cut them in quarters lengthwise. Add the eggs and the other ingredients on top of the lettuce leaves.

TIPS & TRICKS

Be very careful with the knife when you are chopping the vegetables. Ask an adult to help. Hold the knife firmly by the handle and use your other hand to hold the vegetables. Always watch what you are doing, and make sure that your fingertips stay well away from the blade of the knife.

Ingredients

10 fresh large lettuce leaves

1 red pepper

1 cucumber

1 red onion

2 ripe salad tomatoes

2 hard-boiled eggs

¾ cup (200 ml) tuna, preserved in olive oil

12 black olives

salt

3 tablespoons (45 ml) olive oil

Poulet en brochettes

Chicken skewers

Brochettes, or skewers, are a common dish from southern France and the Mediterranean island of Corsica. Skewers are fun to make because you can alternate the meat and other ingredients on the skewers to make each one look different. When cooked, you can slide the ingredients off the skewer with a fork. The grapefruit in this recipe can be replaced with cherry tomatoes or another vegetable.

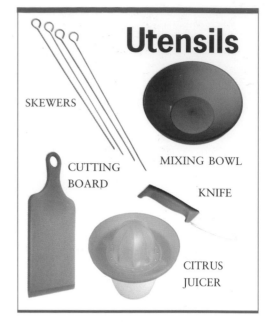

Utensils

SKEWERS

CUTTING BOARD

MIXING BOWL

KNIFE

CITRUS JUICER

1 Place the chicken breasts and pancetta or bacon on a chopping board. Chop them into bite-sized pieces.

2 Cut one of the two grapefruits in half and squeeze out the juice using a citrus juicer.

3 Beat the grapefruit juice with the olive oil and a little salt and pepper in a bowl. Add the chopped meat and mix well. Set aside to **marinate** for at least 30 minutes. Two hours is even better, if you have the time.

4 Peel the remaining grapefruit, removing as much of the inner skin as possible. Ask an adult to help you use a pointed knife to remove the remaining membrane, or skin covering each wedge.

Ingredients

2 chicken breasts (almost 1 lb/ 400 g)

2 large grapefruit

½ lb (200 g) pancetta or bacon

6 tablespoons (90 ml) olive oil

salt and freshly ground black pepper

TIPS & TRICKS

If using wooden skewers, soak them well in cold water first so they do not burn. These skewers can also be cooked over a barbecue or under the grill in the oven.

5 Stick a piece of chicken onto a skewer, then follow with a piece of pancetta, and then a piece of grapefruit. Repeat until the skewer is full. When all the skewers are ready, place them in a lightly oiled, nonstick skillet over medium to high heat for about 15 minutes. Turn them often during cooking and sprinkle with a little salt. Ask an adult to help you.

La Fête des Rois

La Fête des Rois, or The Feast of the Kings, takes place in France at Epiphany, which is celebrated on January 6. Epiphany is an ancient festival that celebrates the Three Kings who went to worship Jesus at Bethlehem, soon after he was born. In France, a special *galette*, or cake, is baked with a *fève*, or bean hidden inside. Whoever finds the bean in their piece of cake is king for a day. Invite your friends to a party. Bake the *galette* and put a secret mark on top where the bean is located that only you will recognize. Since you are the host, do not take that piece. The youngest guest hides under the table and calls the name of the next person to receive a slice.

Remember to put the bean in the cake mixture.

La galette des Rois

- ½ cup (125 ml) butter
- ¼ cup (125 ml) sugar
- 3 eggs
- ½ cup (125 ml) finely ground almonds
- 2 rounds puff pastry, 12 inch (30 cm) in diameter

Beat the butter and sugar until creamy. Stir in two eggs, one at a time. Then add the almonds. Line a greased springform pan with one of the pastry rounds. Fill with the almond mixture. Beat the remaining egg and brush it over the edges of the pastry in the pan. Place the other pastry round on top and seal well. Use a knife to make patterns in the pastry. Brush the rest of the beaten egg over the top. Bake in a preheated oven at 400°F (200°C) for 30 minutes. Serve warm.

This beautiful painting was painted by the Italian artist, Gentile da Fabriano, in 1423. It shows the Three Kings worshiping the baby Jesus. The Kings traveled from the East to Bethlehem. They followed a bright guiding star.

Buy some colored paper and prepare simple crowns for your guests to wear. Make one extra special crown for the person who finds the bean in their cake.

Hachis Parmentier

Minced meat and potato pie

The combination of minced meat and potato purée is so good that this may become one of your favorite French foods. Potatoes were not always so well liked in France. When Monsieur Parmentier, for whom the dish was named, began growing potatoes in about 1785, no one liked them. Parmentier had to use tricks just to get people to taste them!

Ingredients

2 lb (1 kg) potatoes cooked in their skins

2 cups (500 ml) milk

6 tablespoons (90 ml) butter

10 oz (300 g) cooked meat, or uncooked ground meat

1 large onion

bunch of parsley

salt

dash of freshly grated nutmeg

1 When the potatoes have cooled after cooking, peel the skins with your fingers. Put the potatoes in a bowl.

5 Grease the ovenproof dish with a little butter and cover with a layer of potato. Sprinkle with the parsley, then add the meat. Cover with the remaining potato and top with the butter.

6 Bake in a preheated oven at 400°F (200°C) for 20 minutes.

2 Mash the potatoes with a potato masher. Add half the butter and stir with a whisk or wooden spoon. Gradually add the milk to make a smooth, creamy mixture. Season with salt, pepper, and nutmeg.

TIPS & TRICKS

Remember to turn the oven on about 15 minutes before you finish preparing the pie so that it will be hot when you are ready to cook. Serve the pie at room temperature.

3 Place the meat on a cutting board and chop with a half moon chopper or blend in a food processor until well ground. Chop the onion and cut the parsley into fine bits.

4 Melt half the remaining butter in a skillet and fry the onion and parsley. Add the meat and season with salt and pepper. Cook for 5 minutes over medium heat. Ask an adult to help you when using the stove.

Utensils

POTATO PEELER

HALF-MOON CHOPPER

WHISK

MIXING SPOON

SKILLET (FRYING PAN)

OVENPROOF BAKING DISH

Sole meunière

Butter, lemon, and parsley sole

Sole is so tasty that the ancient Romans called the fish *solea jovis*, or Jupiter's sandal, in honor of one of their gods. Chefs have found many different ways of serving it in French cuisine. This recipe is called *"sole meunière,"* or miller's sole and is dipped in flour and **sautéed** in butter to make a tasty sauce.

Sprinkle the sole with the parsley before serving. Serve hot!

TIPS & TRICKS

Turning the sole in the skillet is a little difficult. Ask an adult to help you with this step. Be sure to take the skillet off the heat while you do it. Any kind of small thin fish or fillet can be used for this recipe.

1 Place the flour in a large flat-bottomed bowl or plate. Dip the sole in it one at a time, making sure they are well coated on both sides.

Depending on the size of your skillet, add half of the butter for two sole or one quarter if only one sole will fit.

2 Melt the butter in a nonstick skillet over low heat. Add a drop of oil to the pan to prevent the butter from burning.

Ingredients

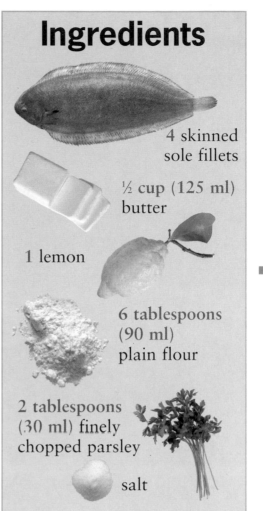

4 skinned sole fillets

½ cup (125 ml) butter

1 lemon

6 tablespoons (90 ml) plain flour

2 tablespoons (30 ml) finely chopped parsley

salt

3 Add the sole to the skillet and cook over low heat. After about 5 minutes, flip the sole with a slotted spatula. Cook for another 5 minutes. Season with salt.

4 While the sole is cooking, squeeze the lemon halves using a citrus juicer.

5 When the sole are almost cooked, pour half the lemon juice over them and cook for 1 more minute. Slip the sole onto a serving dish and cook the rest.

Utensils

SKILLET (FRYING PAN)

SLOTTED SPATULA

CITRUS JUICER

Clafoutis

Cherry tart

This tasty dessert is quick to make and to eat! It is a specialty from the central region of Limousin. Its name comes from a **dialect** word *clafir*, which means "to fill." The original recipe uses whole cherries with their pits, but it is a good idea to remove the pits before you begin, or buy cherries with the pits already removed.

Ingredients

1 lb (450 g) ripe cherries

3 eggs

3 tablespoons (45 ml) icing sugar

¾ cup (200 ml) milk

butter to grease the tart pan

TIPS & TRICKS

If cherries are not in season, replace them with the same quantity of any kind of berry or fruit used in cooking. Always use protective oven mitts when putting things into or taking them out of the oven.

Serve the tart straight from the oven with vanilla ice cream or let it cool and serve with whipped cream.

1 Wash the cherries under cold running water, drain well, and pat dry with a clean cloth. Remove the stems and the pits.

Utensils

FLOUR
SIFTER

CHERRY
PITTER
(OPTIONAL)

EGG BEATER

MIXING BOWL

KITCHEN
SCALE

OVENPROOF
BAKING DISH

2 In a bowl, beat the eggs with 2 tablespoons (30 ml) of icing sugar. Add the flour and milk, a little at a time. Beat continuously until the batter is smooth and fairly liquid.

4 Pour the batter over the cherries. Bake the tart in a preheated oven at 375°F (190°C) for 20 minutes. Remove from the oven and sprinkle with the remaining icing sugar. Bake for 15 minutes more.

3 Butter a tart pan and arrange the cherries evenly in the bottom of the pan. Check that all the cherries are in good condition. Throw out any that are **overripe**.

Tarte aux fraises
Srawberry tart

France is the third largest producer of strawberries in the world. It is not surprising then that the French were the inventors of this delicious tart. Grown in the Rhone Valley, Brittany, and in other areas of France, strawberries are full of vitamins and are actually good for you.

1 Sift the flour into a bowl. Add the butter and work it in with your fingers until the mixture is the consistency of bread crumbs. Stir in the egg yolks, then shape the pastry into a ball. Wrap it in plastic wrap and place in the refrigerator for about 30 minutes.

Ingredients

2½ cups (625 ml) all-purpose/plain flour

½ cup (125 ml) butter

2 egg yolks

5 tablespoons (75 ml) sugar

¾ cup (200 ml) strawberry jam

2 lb (1 kg) clean, fresh strawberries

2 lb (1kg) dried beans

5 **Dilute** the jam with 2–3 tablespoons of warm water. Use a new, clean pastry brush to "paint" the top of the strawberries with the jam. Remove from the pan and serve at room temperature with ice cream or whipped cream.

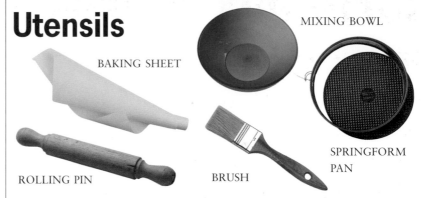

Utensils

BAKING SHEET

MIXING BOWL

ROLLING PIN

BRUSH

SPRINGFORM PAN

2 Sprinke flour on a rolling pin and roll the dough out on a floured work surface until it is about ¼ inch (5 mm) thick.

4 Remove the baked pastry shell from the oven and throw out the paper and beans. Arrange the strawberries, pointed end facing upward on the pastry in the pan.

3 Use the dough to line a buttered and floured 10-inch (26-cm) diameter springform pan. Cover with a sheet of ovenproof paper and fill with the dried beans. Bake in a preheated oven at 350°F (180°C) for about 20 minutes.

TIPS & TRICKS

Be sure to use a springform pan, otherwise it will be hard to get the tart out of the baking pan without breaking it. If strawberries are out of season, replace them with the same quantity of raspberries.

Mousse au chocolat

Chocolate mousse

Soft, fluffy, and sweet, mousse is almost pure chocolate and will be a favorite with your family and friends. Chocolate mousse is one of the easiest and most common French desserts to make. It became a popular treat in the 1970s with the introduction of **nouvelle cuisine**. The best part about this recipe is cleaning up and licking the spoons!

1 Put the chocolate in a small saucepan with the milk and then put the saucepan into a larger pan of cold water. Place over medium heat, and stir until the chocolate melts.

2 In a bowl, beat the **separated** egg yolks with the sugar until they are pale and creamy. Stir it into the melted chocolate.

Utensils

SPATULA

EGG BEATER

SMALL SAUCEPAN

SAUCEPAN

3 Beat the egg whites with a dash of salt until they form stiff peaks. **Fold** the beaten egg whites into the chocolate, taking care that the egg whites do not unstiffen.

4 Beat the cream with an electric or hand held beater until thick. Fold it carefully into the chocolate and egg mixture.

Ingredients

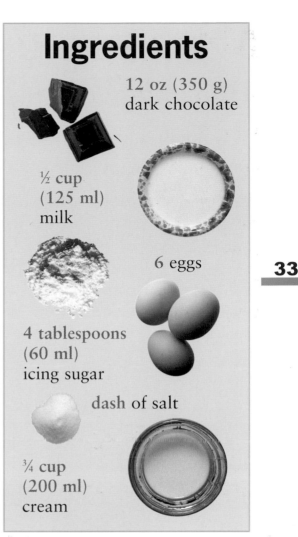

12 oz (350 g)
dark chocolate

½ cup
(125 ml)
milk

6 eggs

4 tablespoons
(60 ml)
icing sugar

dash of salt

¾ cup
(200 ml)
cream

TIPS & TRICKS

When melting the chocolate, be sure to place the saucepans on back burners and keep a firm grip on the handle as you stir. Do not over-whip the cream in step 4, or it will become the same texture as butter.

5 Transfer the mousse mixture into individual dessert dishes or one large serving bowl. Leave in the refrigerator for at least 4 hours before serving. Add whipped cream if desired.

Profiteroles

Chocolate cream puffs

You might have seen this rich-looking dessert in the window of bakeries many times. Now you can make it at home. To make things easier, you can buy the cream puff cases already made. Then just fill them with ice cream, dip them in chocolate, and decorate with whipped cream.

Ingredients

7 oz (200 g) dark chocolate

10 oz (300 g) ready-made cream puff cases

10 oz (300 g) vanilla ice cream

1 cup (250 ml) whipping cream

1 Use a knife to break up the chocolate. Put the chocolate in a small saucepan and then put the bowl into a larger pan of cold water. Place over medium heat, and stir until the chocolate melts.

TIPS & TRICKS

Take the ice cream out of the freezer just before you begin to fill the cream puffs. If you take it out too early it will melt while you work. You can also try filling the cream puffs with vanilla custard or whipped cream instead of the ice cream. You can also add fruit sauce on top of the dessert.

2 Make a small hole in each cream puff case. Using a pastry chef's syringe, fill each one with ice cream.

3 Arrange the filled cream puffs on a round plate one on top of the other in a pyramid shape. Use a little of the chocolate to stick them together.

Place attractive blobs or swirls of cream all over the profiterolle pyramid.

4 Pour the remaining chocloate over the top so that it runs down the sides. Beat the cream until it is thick. Fill the syringe with the whipped cream and decorate the stack of cream puffs.

Utensils

EGG BEATER

KNIFE

PASTRY CHEF'S SYRINGE

SPATULA

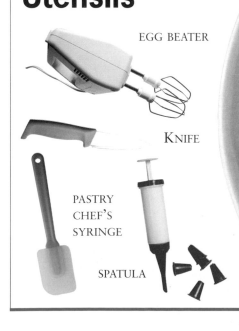

Crème brûlée

Vanilla custard with crusty brown sugar topping

Crème brûlée means burnt custard in the French language, but this dessert is not actually burnt. The brown sugar placed under the grill forms a melt-in-your-mouth crust, which combines well with the creamy vanilla custard underneath. To really enjoy crème brûlée, serve it while it is still a bit warm.

Ingredients

7 egg yolks

2 whole eggs

¾ cup (150 ml) sugar

2 cups (500 ml) fresh cream

⅓ cup (100 ml) milk

4 tablespoons (60 ml) brown sugar

1 In a bowl, beat the separated egg yolks with the sugar until they are pale and creamy.

TIPS & TRICKS

Ask an adult to help you place the roasting pan filled with custard in the oven. You must be careful not to spill water in the oven. When checking to see if it is cooked, and when grilling the sugar, remember to wear thick oven mitts.

2 Heat the cream and milk together. Just before they boil, remove from heat and pour them into the egg and sugar mixture, beating continuously.

To test whether the baked custard is cooked, insert a cake tester or toothpick into the custard. If it comes out dry and clean, the custard is ready.

Utensils

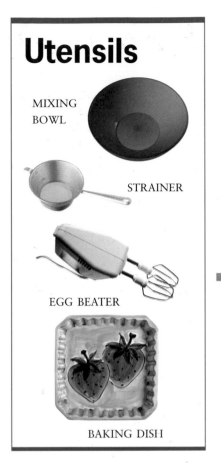

MIXING BOWL

STRAINER

EGG BEATER

BAKING DISH

3 Filter the mixture using a strainer.

4 Pour the mixture into a buttered ovenproof dish. Put the dish in a larger dish or pan, such as a roasting pan, filled with cold water. Place both dishes in a preheated oven at 350°F (180°C), and cook for 1 hour. Ask an adult to help you carry large pans.

5 Remove from the oven and set aside to cool. Sprinkle with the brown sugar and place under the grill for 5 minutes until the sugar is nicely browned and crisp.

Glossary

butler the head male servant of a household, in charge of supervising other servants and serving meals

chop to cut into tiny, fine pieces using a knife or food processor.

consistency the degree of firmness of a mixture of ingredients.

dash to add a small amount of an ingredient to a mixture.

dialect a variation of a language in a particular region

dilute to make a liquid thinner by adding water.

first course the first part of a multiple food dinner.

fold to blend an ingredient into a mixture by very gently turning one part over another.

French cuisine the French style or way of cooking food.

Gruyère cheese a pale yellow Swiss cheese.

ladleful adding the amount of liquid that fills a ladle, a utensil with a cup-shaped bowl.

marinate to soak food in a liquid mixture, usually of vinegar or wine, oil, herbs and spices, for a period of time before cooking.

nouvelle cuisine a style of cooking in the 1970s, using fresh ingredients, a variety of foods, and light sauces, served in a decorative way.

nutritious a food that is healthy to eat and provides a lot of nourishment.

overripe fruit or vegetables that are past their best appearance and texture.

sautéed foods that are cooked or browned in a pan containing a small quantity of butter or oil.

savory something that is pleasant in taste or smell.

separate in cooking, to divide an egg's yolk from its white, both to be used at different stages of a recipe

sift to separate and keep the coarse parts from the fine parts of flour.

skillet a small saucepan with a long handle, or a frying pan.

springform pan a metal cake pan with sides that can be unfastened to take out the cake.

sprinkle to scatter in separate drops.

trim to remove the extra or unwanted parts of a food item.

wedges thick slices.

Index